A Newbies Guide to Using

iMovie

For iPad

Minute Help Guides

Minute Help Press
www.minutehelp.com

Table of Contents

Chapter 1: Introduction

The iMovie app for iPad is a fantastic app that allows you to do two big things with video. With iMovie for iPad, you can create Trailers and Projects, which opens up a world of possibilities for video editing that never existed before. iMovie for the iPad gives you the ability to shoot and edit videos on the go, in a convenient hand held format, and share them with the world. The app gives you a variety of templates that make it easy for even a beginner to create original videos and share them widely. But even video pros find things to like about this app -- it's that powerful. Brave video explorers have created complex and substantial movies, using only this app.

Trailers are slick, ready-made presentations that look like movie trailers. Plug in your home videos and you can create an engaging presentation without advanced directing or editing skills. Projects are more powerful and freeform -- you can literally create any type of video you can imagine, all the way up to making a feature film.

If you've used iMovie on a Mac before, much of what you'll see here will be familiar to you. The addition of a touch screen, however, is a revelation. The visual metaphors that Apple uses for editing video come from old-fashioned film editing suites that edit actual motion pictures. Editing is a physical business and, once you've been able to slide the scenes of your video back and forth with your finger to find the exact edit point you want, you may never want to go back to your Mac.

You can exchange videos from an iPhone or iPod touch, which easily shoots hand held video, if you have one. You can also shoot or edit on your iPad itself. If you have a Mac, you can undertake even more ambitious projects. And, by sharing across the Internet, you can open doors you haven't even imaged yet, all with this simple little app.

Chapter 2: Basics

Using iMovie

One of the easiest ways to get started with creating video in iMovie is to create a Trailer. Trailers work much like the trailers you see when you go to the movies. They mix video clips with text to create an overview of a story, and they use music as a dramatic counterpoint. Instead of trying to show friends hours of home video from your vacation or party, you can use Apple's trailers to easily combine videos in a short format that is enjoyable to watch for friends and family.

One of the great things about working with Trailers is that Apple provides several templates, complete with video footage, so you can see how the videos and music fit together. In the process, you'll also learn some of the gestures you'll use to control iMovie. You'll still use these techniques when you go on to more ambitious projects.

It will probably help to have some video sources available to create your project. iMovie can use pretty much any video that was recorded on your iPad. So, if you've taken vacation or birthday videos with a camera that records in a compatible format, you're all ready. If not, don't worry. You can simply shoot some video with your iPad, directly into iMovie. We'll show you how in a few minutes.

The first time you launch iMovie, it will take you to the My Projects screen, which looks like an old-fashioned movie theater marquee, mounted on a brick wall. As you create various original videos, they will appear on this wall, like movie posters. You can scroll through your projects by swiping to the right or left.

TIP: When you first launch iMovie, it may ask for permission to use your location. Long story short, this feature is helpful in interacting with iPhoto on your Mac, if you use a Mac. If you allow this feature, it will be easier to use iPhoto to import photos and videos from your Mac to your iPad. We recommend you allow this.

Finally, a note: To make this guide easier to read, we'll use the following conventions. Whenever there's a part of the *user interface* that has an official name -- like the Media Library or the My Project screen -- we'll capitalize the name. Whenever it's a part you have to interact with, like the **Play button** or the **Done button**, we'll put that in **boldface**. The first time we use certain technical terms, relating to computer technology or film-making, like *user interface* or *fade*, we'll use *italics*. We'll try to explain all these terms but, if you feel confused, you may want to search on some of these terms.

Making trailers

Remember, trailers are basically templates provided by Apple that allow you to easily insert your own videos into that structure. The timing of the cuts, the placement of titles and the music are all provided in the template. The process is clear and easy, but somewhat rigid. If you want a more freeform video, we'll show you how to create a project later on. But make sure to read this important information too.

Creating a Trailer

Let's start by creating a trailer.

To create a trailer:

Go to the My Projects screen. If you've opened iMovie for the first time, you will probably already go to this screen.

TIP: You must be in landscape (sideways) orientation to use the Trailers interface.

Tap the + **button**.

Tap **New Trailer**.

You'll be taken to a screen that looks like the interior of a movie theater, with a large blank movie screen. Below that, you'll see several small movie screens with titles. Each title will express basic styles such as "Narrative," "Retro," or "Romance."

You can scroll right or left by swiping your finger across these screens.

If you see a style you're interested in, scroll it to the center of the screen and tap it.

The trailer will begin to play on the large movie screen. By seeing the trailers, you can pick the one that's more appropriate to the mood you want to create.

When you find the best trailer for your footage, tap **Create**. Or tap **Cancel** to exit.

How Trailers Work

The secret to trailers is simple. Video editing has a lot to do with timing, and Apple has taken care of that for you. Inside each trailer, there is music, plus a series of *title cards* (text that appears on the screen to give important information) and short video clips that are timed to that music. By putting your videos in place of the videos in the examples, and typing in your own words, you automatically have a pretty slick little project. And it's easy to customize that project to create even more stylistic approaches.

Creating Title Cards

When you tap the **Create** button, you will be taken to the Trailer Editor. On the left hand of the screen you'll see what looks like a notebook. The notebook holds important information film makers use to create their project. The notebook has two tabs, **Outline** and **Storyboard**. By default, you will be in **Outline**.

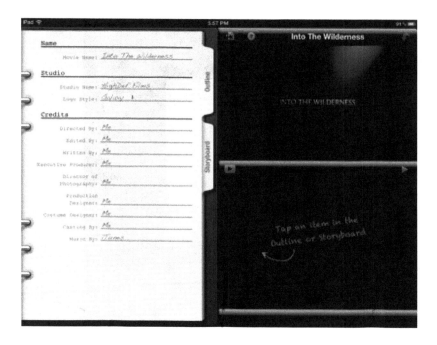

Tap on an entry to select it.

The keyboard will come up. Enter your information for your project.

To close, tap **Done**.

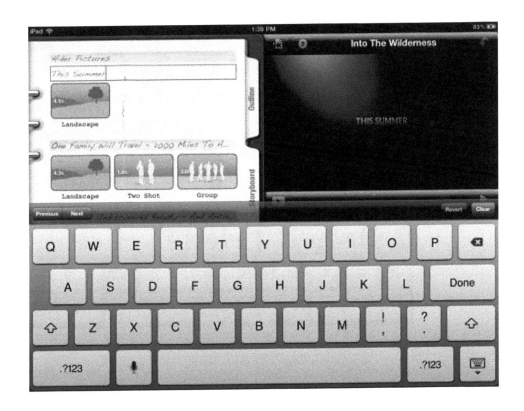

How to edit title cards

If you play any of the trailers, you can see several title cards that come up. To edit those in your trailer, go to **Storyboard**.

You'll see blue bars, containing the current title card text.

Tap in any blue bar to make it editable.

Add your own titles.

Tap **Done**.

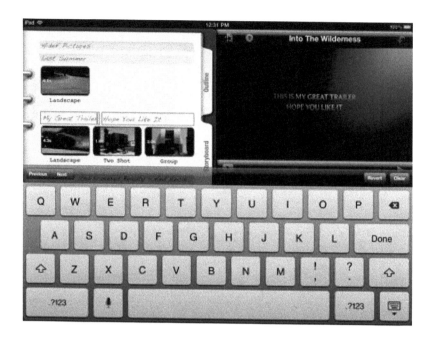

How to put your videos into a trailer

Using the *Storyboard* you can easily select your videos and put them into an already existing trailer template.

To select your videos

On the Notebook display, tap the **Storyboard tab**.

You'll see several sections showing the text from each title card in your trailer, and the text that is currently entered.

TIP: Each panel in the Storyboard represents a scene in your trailer. It contains an illustration with a suggestion of what type of video to use.

Tap a scene to select it.

Your Video Library will pop up in the corner of the screen.

Tap a video to select it and tap the **Blue Arrow icon** to insert that video into that scene.

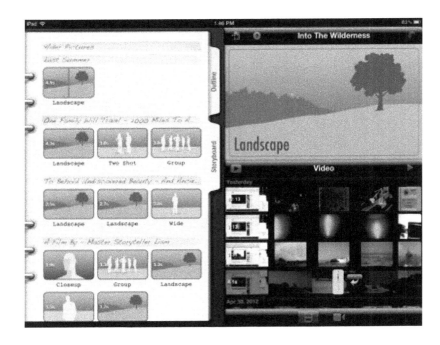

If you don't have any video to edit, you can shoot some right now, by tapping the **Camera** icon at the bottom of the Video Library window.

The panel for that scene changes to show an image from your video.

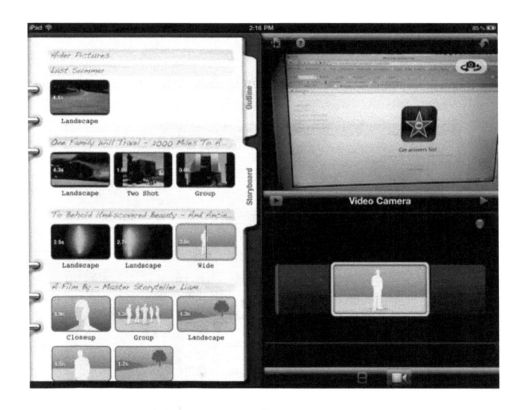

TIP: You can select a video to go into more than one scene, if you have a lot of footage in one particular video that you want to use.

How to select the footage you want to use

The scenes in Apple's trailers are relatively short. Your videos are probably longer, so you'll just want to use the portion that fits best.

Tap a scene that already holds a video to select it.

The Video Library turns into the Edit Shot screen. Your video appears in this screen. A gold rectangle shows the portion of the video that will show in the current scene.

To change what portion of the video to use, scroll right or left until the footage you want scrolls into the gold rectangle.

To see exactly what footage will show, press the **Play button** beneath the golden rectangle.

When you have selected the footage you want, press **Done**.

Repeat this process with every scene in your Storyboard, and soon you'll have a finished trailer!

TIP: An average trailer may contain about 30-40 scenes, so this process may take a while.

TIP: If you like the simplicity of trailers but need more flexibility (to add photos, for instance) and you have a Mac, you can create a trailer and then convert it to a project for more powerful editing features. See the Sharing chapter, and the section called "To send movie to iTunes," for more information about how to transfer your trailer to your Mac and how to open it in iMovie. Once you have followed those steps, you can go to the File menu in the iMovie application and select "Convert to project." This will give you the full capabilities of iMovie. If you want to return the project to your iPad to work on it there, you can do so by following the steps in the Sharing chapter, in the section labeled "To import from iTunes," for more information.

Chapter 3: Advanced Features

Creating a Project

Projects are the heart of iMovie. Unlike trailers, which are highly structured, projects are relatively wide open. You can create your own trailer, if you want, or a commercial, a music video, a short film or even a feature length motion picture.

To create a new project

Go to the My Projects screen.

Tap the + **button**.

Tap **New Project**.

You'll see the Project screen

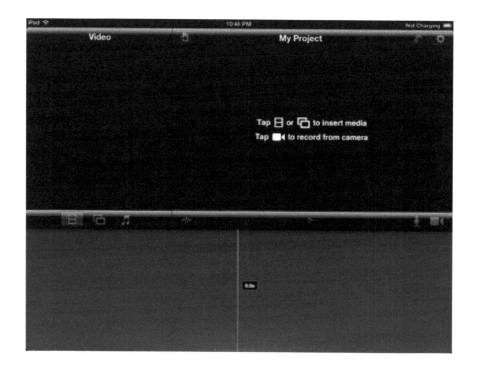

The section in the upper left hand corner is your Media Library, you can use this to look at previews of any videos, photos and audio that you can use in iMovie. For more information about how to make your media files available to iMovie, see the chapter on Sharing. The upper right hand corner of the screen is your Preview window. You can use that to preview video clips and photos from your Media Library, before you put them into your project. Additionally, when you play the project you are working on in the Timeline, playback will show in the Preview window.

To add video to the project

Your Media Library is displayed in the upper left hand corner of the project.

Just tap a video clip and an icon with a **blue arrow** appears, pointing down to the Timeline.

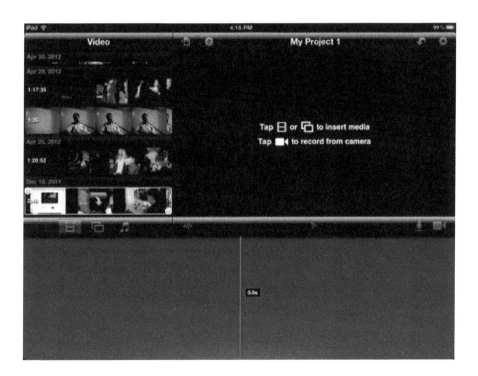

Tap the **blue arrow**.

The clip appears in your Timeline.

To add video to a specific location

If you glance down at the Timeline, you'll see a red vertical line, called the Playhead. Generally, when you insert new video into your project, iMovie will insert it wherever the Playhead is. To move the Playhead, just scroll your project to the right or left.

TIP: If you need an exact idea of where you are in the Timeline, just tap the Timeline, right on the Playhead. A counter will appear in the Preview window with a precise measurement.

To view the video in your project

Press the **Play button** on the Control Strip, just below the Preview window.

To shoot new video

You can also add video to your project by shooting it with your iPad directly from iMovie

Open your project.

In the Edit Screen, look for the **Camera icon**. It's on the right hand side of the Control Strip, just below the Preview Screen.

Your screen will change into a camera, which can be set to record video or take photos.

When you have captured the images you want, tap **Use** to add it to your project or **Cancel**, if you'd like to shoot more.

TIP: Once you add more than one video clip, you'll see small symbols in between each clip, probably with a symbol that looks like two arrows. These small squares are transitions -- the techniques that movies use to get from one scene to another. Usually, one clip will fade out and the next will fade in. iMovie thoughtfully handles the timing automatically to make these fades work but you can customize the transitions if you want. We'll discuss more in the Advanced section.

To add photos to your project

Tap the icon at the bottom of your Media Library that looks like two photo frames.

Your Camera Roll appears.

Tap an album to select it.

Tap a photo to select it.

That photo will be inserted into the Timeline.

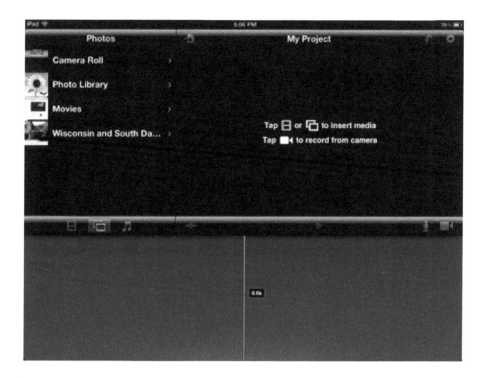

The photo will automatically show in your project as a film clip of about 3-6 seconds. The camera will appear to pan over the image and then zoom in. After the famous documentary director, Apple has dubbed this the Ken Burns effect. To learn how to adjust the length of clip yourself, see "Editing a Project."

To shoot new photos for your project

Follow the instructions above, labeled "To shoot new video," but, when the Camera opens, set the switch to the image of a traditional camera, instead of a movie camera.

To add audio to your project

If you have specific music or sound effects that you want to add to your project's soundtrack, you can access audio files from your Media Library.

To access your audio files

Go to the Edit Screen for the project that you want to add audio to.

In your Media Library (in the upper left hand corner), tap the blue icon that looks like musical notes.

Your Audio Library opens.

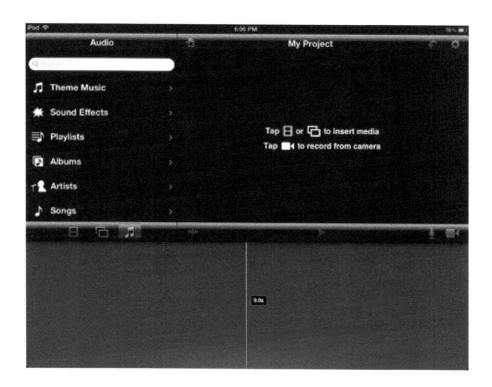

You will be able to select Apple-provided **Theme Music** or **Sound Effects** simply by tapping those names. To preview these audio tracks, press the **Play button** to the right of the audio track's name.

Also, by tapping **Playlist** in your Audio Library, you can access any songs, or other audio files, that you have in your iTunes library. The additional selections, **Albums**, **Artists** and **Songs**, also access your iTunes library in the same way iTunes itself does.

To add audio files to your project

Tap on the name of the audio file you want to use.

A **Green bar** will be added to your project in the Timeline, representing your audio track.

By default, if your music is shorter than the video, the music will play as a continuous loop for the length of the video, if you want to turn looping off, tap the **Project Settings icon** in the upper right hand corner.

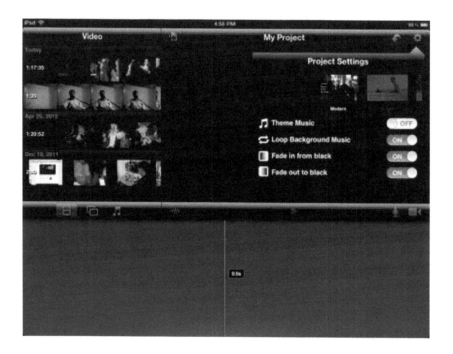

TIP: You must disable looping to use more than one audio track in your project.

If you do want to add additional music, just select it in the manner described above. It will be added at the end of your current audio track.

TIP: When you add additional music, iMovie automatically places it at the end of the existing soundtrack.

To adjust the volume of your audio track

Tap your audio track's **Green bar** to select it.

Double tap the **Green bar** to open the **Audio Clip Settings** window.

Adjust the volume with the **Slider**, or use the switch to turn sound **On** and **Off**.

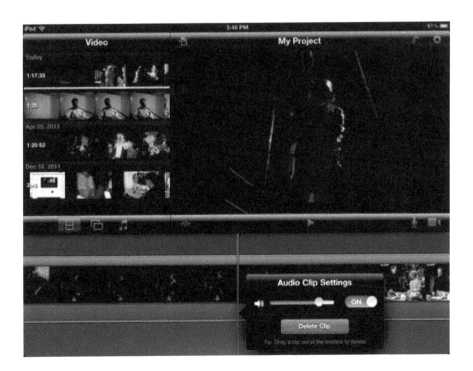

TIP: To make a music video, it may be easier to place the audio file first, and then insert your video clips at appropriate sections timed to the music changes.

How to perform basic edits to your project

Obviously, it's unlikely that every element of your project will fit together perfectly. Editing is a key part of making movies and iMovie has simple, elegant ways to perform a lot of sophisticated editing and effects for your movie. We'll go over these in detail, in the next section, but if you're the type who likes to charge ahead, or you already have a project that you're in a hurry to work on, we'll cover a couple of the most common types of edits here:

To adjust the length of a clip

To adjust the length of a clip, tap it in the Timeline.

Two yellow "handles" will appear on either end of the clip you have selected.

Touch either end of the clip and hold your finger down on it, as you slide it to the right or left.

Moving the handle in, toward the center of the clip, with shorten the length.

The footage you trim is not destroyed by this technique, if there is additional footage in the clip that is not being shown, dragging the handles out will add that footage to the scene.

To move a clip

If you would like to change the order of a clip, touch and hold it until it appears to "pop up" out of the Timeline.

Holding your finger down, drag the clip to its new location and release it.

To delete a clip

To delete a clip, follow the instructions for moving a clip, directly above. But, when the clip has popped up, instead of dragging the clip to a new location, drag it off the Timeline.

To resize the Timeline

When you are trying to move or adjust clips, sometimes it would be convenient for the Timeline to be longer -- to show more accuracy and detail -- or smaller -- so you can see more of the Timeline.

To make the Timeline smaller, place your thumb and first finger on the Timeline and make a pinching gesture, to bring your fingers together.

To make the Timeline larger, use the opposite gesture. Place your fingers together on he Timeline and lowly spread them apart.

To undo an edit

It's always important to be able to undo a change when you are making edits. To undo an action, simply shake your iPad gently. The Undo menu will appear on your screen.

As you can imagine, putting images and audio tracks together is certainly the core of creating any video project. However, that's only the beginning. iMovie offers a variety of powerful editing tools that allow you to refine your project, and turn your media into something you'll be proud to share. The next section goes into much more detail about how to take control of your iMovie project.

Editing a Project

The biggest difference between a trailer and a project is that a project can literally be anything. You have a great deal of control over what clips you use, when you use them and what kind of audio plays during your project. You can actually make a feature length movie on your iPad if you want to, although it might be a bit of a challenge. You'll bring all your media (videos, photos and music) together during editing, to put them into a shape your imagination desires.

TIP: Be patient. Video clips contain a lot of data and, no matter how powerful the iPad is, it's not as powerful as the type of top-of-the-line computers professionals use to edit video. Sometimes it may take iMovie several seconds to perform even a simple task, if you're working with a big enough file. If you find iMovie is responding slowly, make sure to give it a little extra time to process each change. If you have a Mac, you may want to consider dividing larger projects into several small projects and then exporting them to iMovie on your computer to combine them. We'll discuss how to export iMovie projects and trailers in the chapter called Sharing.

To edit your project

If your project is not already open, go to the My Projects screen, select your project and open it.

You'll see the editing screen. There are three major components. In the upper left hand corner is the Media Library. The upper right hand corner shows your project in the Preview screen. Below it is the Timeline.

Remember that we've already discussed some basic editing techniques in the previous section, "How to perform basic edits to your project." We've already discussed how to adjust the size of a clip, move a clip, delete a clip, resize the Timeline, and undo an edit. If you haven't read it, or have forgotten, you should probably go back and look at that information now. After you've done that, we'll go ahead and add in several techniques that may be useful to you.

To split a clip

If your project is not already open, go to the My Projects screen, select your project and open it.

If you have a long video clip that you want to use in more than one section, it may be helpful to split it. To split your clip, scroll the Timeline until the Playhead is over the point where you want to split.

Tap the clip to select it.

Place your finger on the Playhead and, without lifting, drag your finger down the Playhead, through the clip.

The clip will split at that point.

To add a freeze frame your clip

Scroll right or left in the Timeline until the Playhead is at the specific image, or *frame*, that you want to use as a freeze frame.

Tap the clip to select it.

Place your finger on the frame and swipe up.

A freeze frame of the image will be inserted at the Playhead.

To rotate a clip

To achieve certain kinds of effects, clever filmmakers have been known to show images sideways or upside down. This process is easy in iMovie.

Scroll the Timeline right or left until you see the clip you want to rotate in the Preview window.

In the Preview window, place your thumb and forefinger on the clip close together, as if you have just made a pinching motion, and rotate your fingers either clockwise or counterclockwise. The image will rotate 90 degrees in the direction you turned.

If needed, repeat the process until the desired rotation is achieved.

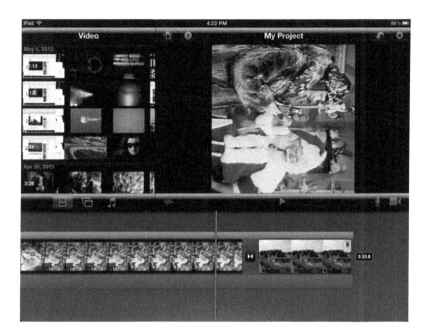

To jump to the beginning or end of a project

To quickly navigate to the project tap and hold your finger at the point where the right end of the video in the Timeline meets the edge of the screen.

Working with themes

Themes are a useful feature that applies to projects. They work very much like some of the features from trailers. Basically, they combine a specific style of title cards, music and transitions that you can easily apply to your project. You can change the theme that is currently applied to your projects, and these elements will all change.

The default theme that iMovie applies to all projects is called Modern. To see the other themes that are available, and choose another if you'd like, just press the **Project Settings icon** in the upper right hand corner of the screen.

To add titles

One feature of themes is the ability to type in text that will show when a particular clip or photo is displayed. To add a title, scroll through the Timeline until you see the clip or photo you would like to title.

Double tap the video or photo.

The Clip Settings window appears

Tap **Title Styles** and select a style.

*TIP: The style names -- **Opening**, **Middle**, and **Ending** are just helpful suggestions. You can use any style, anywhere you want.*

When you select a title style, iMovie will add a text box to the image in the Preview window.

Tap in that text box to call up the keyboard.

Type in whatever information you want to add to your project.

Tap **Done**.

To edit the title

Scroll through your project until you reach the frames where the title appears.

Tap the text box, in the Preview window.

Edit normally when the keyboard appears.

To remove the title

Scroll right or left in the Timeline until you find the clip you want to edit.

Double tap the clip to call up the Clip Settings window.

Tap **Title Style**.

Tap **None**.

Working with transitions

We've already mentioned that iMovie automatically sets transitions between video clips. In the default theme, Modern, iMovie will fade out at the end of each clip and fade in at the beginning of the next clip. For your project, you may want different kinds of transitions, or no transitions.

To edit transitions

In the Timeline, scroll right or left until you reach the transition you want to edit

Double tap the transition you want to edit.

The Transition Settings window opens.

You can choose **None** to create a transition where one clip ends and the next begins immediately, called a *cut*.

You can choose **Cross Dissolve** to have one clip fade out, while the next clip fades in.

You can choose **Theme** to get a special transition, designed by Apple to work with your theme.

For the **Cross Dissolve** and **Theme** settings, you can also choose a duration for the fade.

Chapter 4: Sharing

Creating your new video masterwork wouldn't be very satisfying if you couldn't share it with others. Happily, iMovie comes with a variety of ways you can easily let friends, family, or colleagues view your creations.

Also, you'll probably want to take advantage of some of the features iMovie provides to let you import and export files to a Mac, or other iOS devices. This comes in handy as you gather video and audio clips for your project or trailer, and is a great way to back up your important work

Sharing a video

You can easily share your video to a variety of other programs, and to various websites, just by scrolling to the project or trailer you wish to select on the Marquee screen and tapping the **Share icon**. It looks like a movie screen with an arrow pointing to the right. It's third from the right, along the bottom of the screen. The Share menu will open. You can share to the Camera Roll, YouTube, Facebook, Vimeo, CNN Report, or send your project to iTunes.

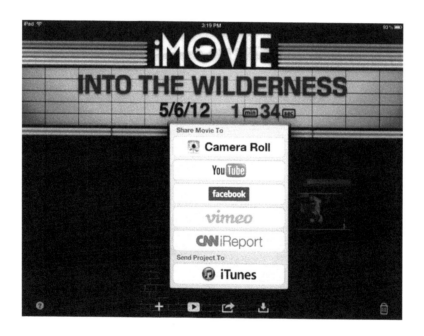

To share your video with the Camera Roll.

Go to the My Projects screen

Scroll to the project you want to share.

Tap the **Share button**.

Tap **Camera Roll**.

Select what size file you want to export.

TIP: Smaller movies are faster to upload and download, so they're good for the internet. HD files are larger, but offer more detail on a big screen like your computer monitor or TV.

When the video has been shared to the Camera Roll, you can go to the Photo app on your iPhone where you can e-mail it. You can connect your iPhone to another computer running iPhoto (or compatible software) and share by syncing the two devices.

TIP: The Camera Roll method exports a version of the completed video, not an iMovie Trailer or Project. To share your actual working project, see "Send to iTunes," below.

To import photos and videos with your Camera Roll

This small section can conceivably save you a lot of frustration, because some of the information is not very intuitive. If you want to import an iMovie project to your iPad, you use iTunes (see "To import from iTunes," below, for more information). However, if you have other videos or photos on your computer that you would like to use in your iMovie project, you import those into your iPad using the Camera Roll.

For this technique, you simply add the photos or videos you want to share to iPhoto, or some iPhoto compatible application, and sync iPhoto to your iPad in the usual way. However, because videos are so large, the default setting is not to sync them from your computer to your iPad.

To change this setting, attach your iPad to your computer and launch iTunes on your computer.

Select the device in the left hand menu in iTunes.

At the top of the iTunes window, select Photos.

If the option labeled Include videos is not selected, select it.

Sync your device normally.

The files you just synced will now be available from iMovie's Media Library

TIP: If you're relatively new to video file formats, there's another frustration to be aware of here. The iMovie app is optimized to use photos and video shot by the iPad or other iOS devices. It will usually work perfectly with those files. Now, because these devices usually create a file using Apple's QuickTime format (the file has a suffix of ".mov"), you might think you could use other QuickTime movies as source clips as well. iMovie also recognizes MP4 files, which are very common on the Internet, and you might think you could import those files as well.

However, that's not always the case. The explanation is pretty complex but let's summarize it this way -- videos usually contain a lot of data, about pictures, sound and information that helps your device understand what data it's looking at, and how to sync it for playback. It's those details that have to match, or iMovie can't use the files. Many times, you'll get lucky and find footage you can use. It's impossible to predict, though. If you're a savvy user, you can convert the files and alter those details so iMovie can use the video clips, but that's a topic for another book.

To share to YouTube

Follow the directions above, but tap **YouTube**.

Enter your YouTube username and password.

Tap **Sign In**.

Tap **Title** and **Description** to add information.

If desired, select a **Category** and add **Tags**.

To enter multiple tags, just tap **Return** after each tag.

Select what size file you want to export.

Select a privacy setting.

Add **Location** information, if desired.

Tap **Share**.

To share to Facebook

Follow the instructions above but select **Facebook**.

Enter your Facebook username and password.

Tap **Sign In**.

Tap **Title** and **Description** to add information.

Select what size file you want to export.

Select a privacy setting.

Tap **Share**.

To share to Vimeo

Follow the instructions above but select **Vimeo**.

Enter your Facebook username and password.

Tap **Sign In**.

Tap **Title** and **Description** to add information.

If desired, select a **Category** and add **Tags**.

To enter multiple tags, just tap **Return** after each tag.

Select what size file you want to export.

Select a privacy setting.

Tap **Share**.

To share to CNN iReport

Follow the directions above, but tap **CNN iReport**.

Enter your YouTube username and password.

Tap **Sign In**.

Tap **Subject** and **Body** to add information.

If desired, select a **Category** and add **Tags**.

To enter multiple tags, just tap **Return** after each tag.

Select what size file you want to export.

Tap **Share**.

To send movie to iTunes

You must use iTunes to share your iMovie project with your Mac or Windows computer, or with other iOS devices. It's a great way to back up your project -- iTunes makes a copy of the project, and your original remains on your iPad.

Follow the directions above, but tap **Send to iTunes**.

When you see a notification that export is complete, tap **OK**.

Connect your iPad to your computer.

Open iTunes on your computer.

In the left hand menu of iTunes, select your device.

At the top of the iTunes window, select **Apps**.

Scroll down until you see a section called File Sharing.

Select **iMovie**.

Select the name of the file you just exported from your iPad.

Click **Save to** and select a location on your computer to save the file.

To import from iTunes

If you have a Mac, you can open your iMovie for iPad file in iMovie on your computer, if you'd like to do additional editing, once you have exported a file to your computer. Otherwise, you may want to share it with another iOS device that also has iMovie installed.

Connect your iOS to your computer.

Open iTunes on your computer.

In the left hand menu of iTunes, select your device.

At the top of the iTunes window, select **Apps**.

Scroll down until you see a section called File Sharing.

Select **iMovie**.

Select the name of the file you want to import.

You will see a confirmation screen in iMovie

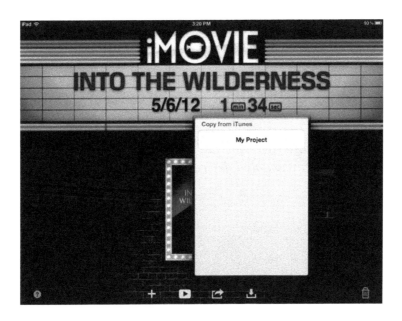

TIP: If you are using a Mac, you can now use iMovie on your Mac to open the file you have saved, to do more editing. If you have Apple's powerful, professional Final Cut movie making software, you can also open the files with that.

To stream your movie to your Apple TV

Apple TV users are probably familiar with many uses of AirPlay -- Apple's technology to stream video from your iTunes library to not only Apple TV, but also other audio and video equipment from several major manufacturers. Well, that technology can also be used to stream your iMovie creation to your TV.

Turn on your Apple TV and your HDTV.

TIP: Your Apple TV and your iPad must be connected to the same wireless network.

Go to the My Projects screen (the Marquee screen) and scroll to the project or trailer you want to stream.

Press the **Play button** on the My Projects screen.

When the video begins to play on your iPad, tap the **AirPlay button**.

When you are finished viewing, tap **Done** in the upper left corner of your iPad's screen.

TIP: If this is the first time you have used AirPlay, the system may take a few moments to prepare the video and to detect any AirPlay-enabled devices on your network.

Chapter 5: Conclusion

It's truly remarkable what you can accomplish using a small hand held device, and an inexpensive software app. If you are a blogger, a journalist or just a creative soul, you now have the power to create relatively sophisticated movies, right from the site of whatever event you are recording. For more casual users, you can create a video of your family vacation and share it with friends before you even come home. A group of daring film makers have already vowed to create an entire feature film using only iMovie for iPad. With iMovie, Apple has achieved what they do best -- creating powerful tools that you can use, without constantly trying to figure out how to use them. With those tools and this quick guide, you're ready to start making movies right away.

About Minute Help Press

Minute Help Press is building a library of books for people with only minutes to spare. Follow @minutehelp on Twitter to receive the latest information about free and paid publications from Minute Help Press, or visit minutehelp.com

www.ingramcontent.com/pod-product-compliance
Lightning Source LLC
Chambersburg PA
CBHW060506060326
40689CB00020B/4652